The UNFORGETTABLE SEASON

The Story of
JOE DiMAGGIO,
TED WILLIAMS
and the
RECORD-SETTING
SUMMER OF '41

PHIL BILDNER *illustrated by* **S. D. SCHINDLER**

PUFFIN BOOKS • **AN IMPRINT OF PENGUIN GROUP (USA)**

TO ALEX,
A LIFELONG
RED SOX FAN;
TO SAM,
A LIFELONG
YANKEES FAN;
AND TO
THE KIDS AND
LIBRARIANS OF
THE STATE OF TEXAS.
WITHOUT YOU,
I COULDN'T DO THIS.
—P.B.

PUFFIN BOOKS
An imprint of Penguin Young Readers Group
Published by the Penguin Group
Penguin Group (USA)
375 Hudson Street
New York, New York 10014, U.S.A.

USA / Canada / UK / Ireland / Australia / New Zealand / India / South Africa / China
Penguin Books Ltd, Registered Offices: 80 Strand, London WC2R 0RL, England

For more information about the Penguin Group visit www.penguin.com

First published in the United States of America by G. P. Putnam's Sons, a division of Penguin Young Readers Group, 2011
Published by Puffin Books, an imprint of Penguin Young Readers Group, 2014

Text copyright © Phil Bildner, 2011
Illustrations copyright © S. D. Schindler, 2011
Lyrics and music to "Joltin' Joe DiMaggio" by Alan Courtney and Benjamin Homer. All rights reserved.

THE LIBRARY OF CONGRESS HAS CATALOGED THE G. P. PUTNAM'S SONS EDITION AS FOLLOWS:
Bildner, Phil. The unforgettable season : the story of Joe DiMaggio, Ted Williams and the record-setting summer of '41 / Phil Bildner; illustrated by S. D. Schindler.   p. cm.   ISBN 978-0-399-25501-4 (hardcover)   1. Baseball—United States—History—20th century. 2. Baseball players—United States. 3. DiMaggio, Joe, 1914–1999. 4. Williams, Ted, 1918–2002. I. Title.   GV863.A1B53 2011   796.357 64097309044—dc22   2010007382

Puffin Books ISBN 978-0-14-751055-6

Manufactured in China

10 9 8 7 6 5 4 3 2 1

The publisher does not have any control over and does not assume any responsibility for author or third-party websites or their content.

SOURCES
Chass, Murray. "1941: A Streak for the Ages." SouthCoastToday.com,
    http://archive.southcoasttoday.com/daily/03-99/03-09-99/d01sp116.htm.
Cramer, Richard Ben. *Joe DiMaggio: The Hero's Life*. New York: Simon & Schuster, 2001.
Halberstam, David. *The Teammates: A Portrait of a Friendship*. New York: Hyperion, 2004.
Katz, Harry, Frank Ceresi, Phil Michel, Wilson McBee and Susan Reyburn.
    Baseball Americana: Treasures from the Library of Congress. New York: Smithsonian Books, 2009.
Leiker, Ken, Alan Schwarz and Mark Vancil. *Red Sox: A Retrospective of Boston Baseball*.
    New York: Sterling Books, 2005.
Ward, Geoffrey C., and Ken Burns. *Baseball: An Illustrated History*. New York: Knopf, 1994.
Joe DiMaggio's official website: www.joedimaggio.com
Ted Williams' official website: www.tedwilliams.com

Baseball fans know their numbers.

Whether they root for the Reds, Royals, Rockies or Rays, those who love America's national pastime have always been aware of the time-tested measuring sticks inscribed in the record books.

60. 2,130. 714.

Yes, baseball fans know their numbers. And they also know that all records—even the unbreakable ones—will one day fall. But two of the biggest still have not. And incredibly, these two records were both set in 1941, during one unforgettable season.

JOE DiMAGGIO played the game with the grace of a clipper ship, so they called him the Yankee Clipper. Yet even though he'd already led the New York Yankees to four World Series titles, Joe DiMaggio still hadn't won over the hearts of the Yankee faithful. Early in his career, he'd dared to ask for a pay raise, and as a result, New Yorkers thought he was selfish and ungrateful. Some even booed when he stepped onto the field.

One month into the '41 season, the New York Yankees were in the middle of an awful slump. "Yank Attack Weakest in Years" screamed the headline in *The New York Journal-American*.

Then, on Thursday, May 15, Joe stroked a base hit off Chicago White Sox pitcher Eddie Smith. With one swing of the bat, the Yankees' entire season turned around. For on that warm spring afternoon in the Bronx, *the Streak* began.

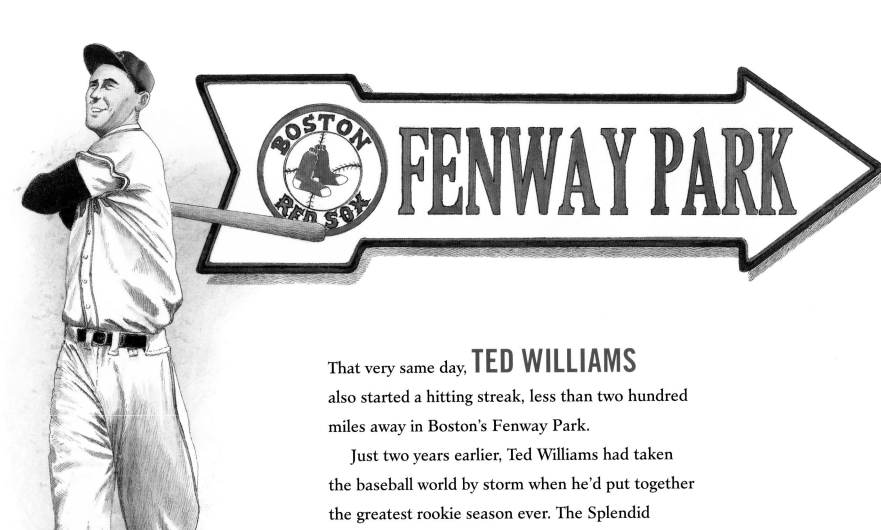

That very same day, **TED WILLIAMS** also started a hitting streak, less than two hundred miles away in Boston's Fenway Park.

Just two years earlier, Ted Williams had taken the baseball world by storm when he'd put together the greatest rookie season ever. The Splendid Splinter—which he was called because he was tall and slender like a piece of wood—blasted thirty-one home runs and hit a whopping .327.

Yet by 1941, many in Red Sox Nation had grown tired of the prickly outfielder. Some fans thought he was lazy and didn't always try his hardest. They suggested he be traded to another team, even to the rival Yankees.

But from the middle of May to the middle of June, Ted hit in every single game, raising his batting average to .430. At the time, no player had hit above .400 for an entire season in more than ten years, which many baseball experts considered the greatest hitting feat in all of baseball.

JOE DiMAGGIO's streak was still going strong when Ted's streak ended on June 8 after 23 games. Better yet, Joe's incredible run had propelled the Yankees into first place.

Day after day, "Joltin' Joe"—another nickname, because he smacked the ball so hard, it was like an electric jolt—hit and hit and hit. Twenty-eight straight games. Twenty-nine games. Thirty games, which broke the all-time Yankees team record.

On front stoops and street corners all over the Bronx, and on playgrounds and school yards throughout Joe's hometown of San Francisco, the same question was being asked:

"Did he get a hit?"

Les Brown and His Orchestra even recorded a song about the Streak. Night and day, "Joltin' Joe DiMaggio" was heard on the radio.

"From coast to coast, that's all you hear
Of Joe the one-man show.
He's glorified the horsehide sphere,
Joltin' Joe DiMaggio."

On June 28, the Yankees traveled to Philadelphia's Shibe Park to face the Athletics. Before the game, A's pitcher Johnny Babich boasted, "I know how to handle DiMaggio."

Babich vowed to stop Joe's streak with a simple strategy: He wouldn't give the Yankee Clipper anything good to hit. If Babich walked Joe in each at bat, the Streak would be over.

But in the middle of the game, Joe swung at a pitch far out of the strike zone. **Smack!**

Base hit up the middle!

Joltin' Joe hit the ball so hard, Babich never
even saw it pass right between his own legs!

Meanwhile, during a Sunday afternoon doubleheader in Boston, **TED WILLIAMS** smacked four hits and scored four runs as the Red Sox swept Chicago. A day later, the Detroit Tigers came to town for a twin bill, and once again, Ted put on a hitting show. In the first game, he belted a game-winning home run, and during the nightcap, he reached base six times, keeping his average above the magic .400 mark.

"You're tearing the cover off the ball, Teddy," said teammate Dom DiMaggio, who knew better than anyone. Not only did he play alongside Ted in the Red Sox outfield, but he also happened to be Joe DiMaggio's little brother. "Keep it up, and you'll hit .400 for the season!"

"That's what those boys are writing in the papers, Dommie," Williams replied. "But I'll let my timber do the talking."

A week before the All-Star break, **JOE DiMAGGIO** and the Yankees faced the Washington Senators in a doubleheader. If Joe managed to get a hit in both games, he'd break George Sisler's American League record of 41 games.

That afternoon, none of Joe's teammates dared mention the Streak to him, fearing they could accidentally jinx him.

They didn't have to worry: In the opener, Joe stroked a double to left field, tying the all-time mark. With just one hit in the nightcap, the record would be his.

But between games, the unthinkable happened.

"Where's my bat?" Joe asked fellow slugger Tommy Henrich. "It was just right."

A Yankees fan—who really couldn't have been much of a fan at all—had stolen it!

Each time the Yankee Clipper stepped to the plate, he couldn't hit a lick. Waiting in the on-deck circle late in the game, Joe realized he only had one more chance. Henrich came over and held out his lumber.

"This bat has a hit in it," Henrich said.

"It looks familiar," Joe said.

"It should," Henrich replied. "It's one of yours. You lent this one to me a few weeks ago when I was in a slump."

Wagging his own bat, Joltin' Joe stepped to the plate
and smacked a single, setting the American League record.
Afterward, George Sisler sent Joe a telegram.
"I'm glad a real hitter broke it. Keep it up."

The next week was the All-Star Game in Detroit. For a change, **TED** and **JOE** would hit together, back-to-back in the American League lineup, and play side by side in the same outfield. From the Atlantic to the Pacific, people tuned their radios to the midsummer classic.

Down by two runs in the bottom of the ninth, the American Leaguers loaded the bases. Joe stepped to the plate with the chance to be a hero and win the game with a hit. Instead, he rapped a sure-fire double-play ball. Luckily, the second baseman's relay throw to first base sailed wide. Joe was safe, and one run scored, but the American League was still down by one.

Up to the plate stepped TED WILLIAMS, the Splendid Splinter.
Boom!

The ball soared high and deep down the right-field line. Without a doubt, the ball was going to land in the upper deck of Briggs Stadium. But would it stay fair?

Yes! Ted had hit the game-winning three-run home run!

Ted was mobbed at home plate by his fellow All-Stars. The first to greet him was his Yankee rival and friend, Joe DiMaggio.

"The greatest thrill of my life!" Ted exclaimed when he reached the dugout.

49 GAMES

50 GAMES

51 GAMES

52 GAMES

After the All-Star break, **JOLTIN' JOE** picked up where he left off. His record-setting hitting streak rolled on.

Radio broadcasts were interrupted for "DiMag Bulletins."

During long meetings at the Capitol, congressmen waited for the latest DiMaggio updates.

How long could he keep it going?

On a muggy night in Cleveland, Joe went hitless through the first
seven innings of the game against the Indians. With the bases
loaded in the top of the eighth, the Yankee Clipper came up
to bat with one final chance to keep the Streak alive.
The vendors stopped selling peanuts and ice cream,
and the sellout crowd that packed Municipal Stadium
stood and cheered. Even the Cleveland fans waved
signs supporting Joe.

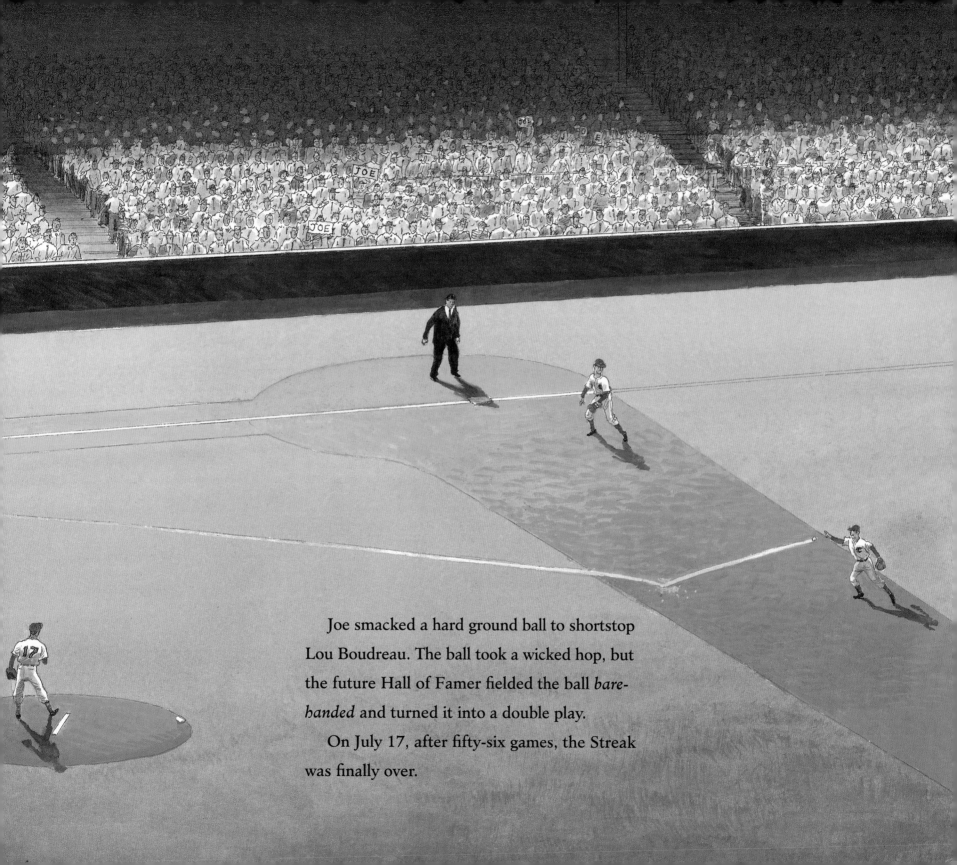

Joe smacked a hard ground ball to shortstop Lou Boudreau. The ball took a wicked hop, but the future Hall of Famer fielded the ball *bare-handed* and turned it into a double play.

On July 17, after fifty-six games, the Streak was finally over.

"I'm not happy that I failed to get a hit," Joe told reporters after the game. "I guess relieved would be a better word. Although I haven't been under much strain, there always was a little pressure until I got a hit."

Almost instantly, the baseball world turned to **TED WILLIAMS**. Up in Boston, the Splendid Splinter was sizzling through the hot summer months, batting .429 in July and .402 in August. During the last week of the season, the Red Sox traveled to Washington for a series against the Senators. But in those three games, Ted managed just two hits in eleven trips to the plate.

On the season's final day, heading into a doubleheader against the Athletics, his batting average had dipped to .39955.

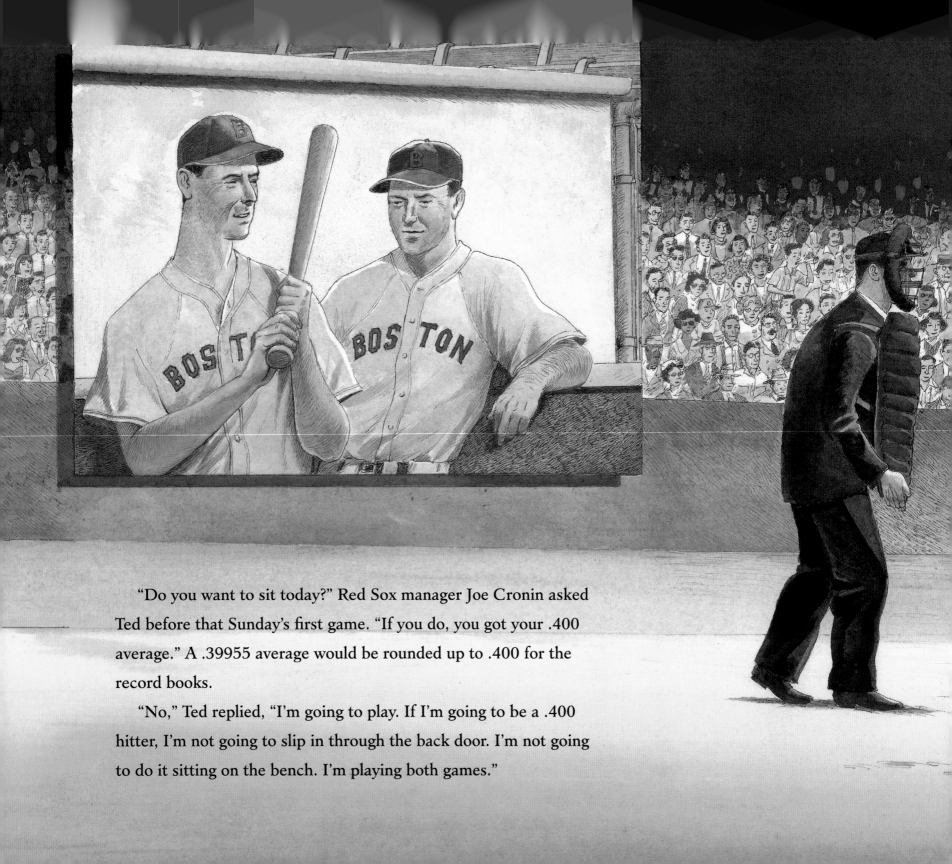

"Do you want to sit today?" Red Sox manager Joe Cronin asked Ted before that Sunday's first game. "If you do, you got your .400 average." A .39955 average would be rounded up to .400 for the record books.

"No," Ted replied, "I'm going to play. If I'm going to be a .400 hitter, I'm not going to slip in through the back door. I'm not going to do it sitting on the bench. I'm playing both games."

Once the first game started, there was no doubt about Ted reaching the milestone.

Ted went four-for-five in the first game, and then in the nightcap, he added two more hits. In his last at bat of the season, the Splendid Splinter smacked a double that rocketed off the loudspeaker horns atop the outfield wall and ricocheted all the way back to the infield!

Ted finished the season batting a whopping .406. He'd done it!

"What a thrill!" Williams declared afterward in the clubhouse. "I wasn't saying anything about it before the game, but I never wanted anything harder in my life."

Seven decades have now passed

and not a single player since Joe DiMaggio has come close to hitting in fifty-six straight games. Only Pete Rose managed to get within a dozen games of Joe's record, hitting in forty-four straight in 1978.

Since Ted Williams, no one has approached batting .400 in a single season either. In the strike-shortened 1994 season, Tony Gwynn hit .394, and in 1980, George Brett batted .390, yet in the end, neither could reach the mark.

TONY GWYNN

GEORGE BRETT

But the next time you visit the ballpark or tune to a game on television, keep your eyes wide open. Because even though it's been more than seventy years since Ted Williams and Joe DiMaggio put on their hitting show for the ages, you never know when a player just might start a quest to bat .400 or begin a record-breaking hitting streak.

It could be this baseball season, or perhaps next year, but one day there will be another season as unforgettable as 1941.

Only nobody knows when.

Baseball by the Numbers

60. In 1927, Babe Ruth hit a record 60 home runs in a single season. Many people thought the number would never be matched. But then, in 1961, Roger Maris hit 61.

2,130. The number of consecutive games the Iron Horse, Lou Gehrig, played for the New York Yankees. No one thought that record could be surpassed. But then, more than a half a century later, it was, when the great Cal Ripken, Jr. played 2,632 games in a row.

714. For decades, whenever anyone heard the number 714, they again thought of Babe Ruth and his lifetime home run total, more than any other player in history. Then that number changed to 755, when Hank Aaron set the new lifetime record.

LOU GEHRIG

CAL RIPKEN, JR.

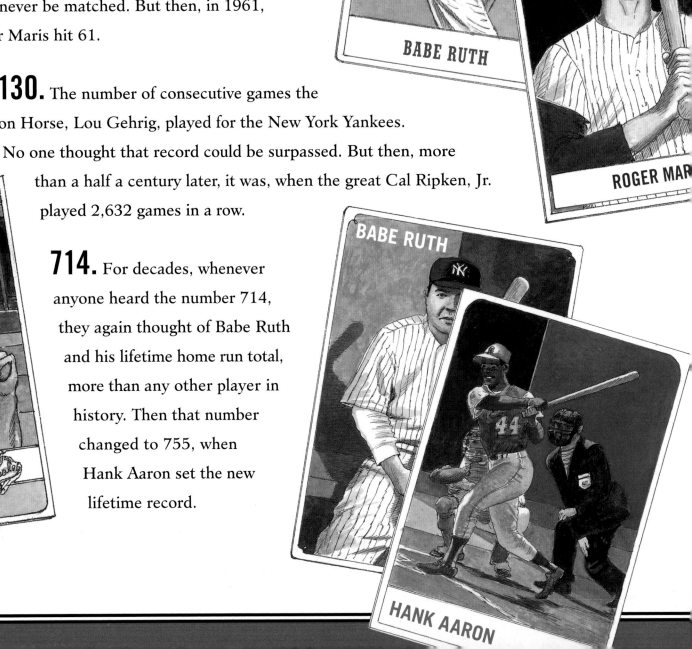

BABE RUTH

ROGER MAR

BABE RUTH

HANK AARON